THE CHANGING CLIMATE

CONTENTS

written and illustrated by Jon Hughes

A WARMING WORLD

The year 2016 was the hottest ever recorded. But one year of hot weather does not mean the world is getting warmer. For the last fifty years, scientists from all over the world have been trying to find out what is really happening. They have been taking measurements of the winds and the weather from satellites in space. They have taken measurements from deep down in the ice of the North and South Poles. They have measured rocks on the surface and deep inside the Earth. They have also measured the temperature of the seas and oceans. Scientists have discovered that the Earth is warming much faster than anyone had thought.

When scientists talk about the weather, they mean the weather that happens each day. However 'climate' describes what people expect the weather to be like in a particular place at a particular time of the year. Previous weather conditions establish the normal pattern. Climate changes mean that the world is getting hotter. But this does not mean that the climate will get warmer everywhere.

pollution covering a city

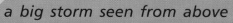

a big storm seen from above

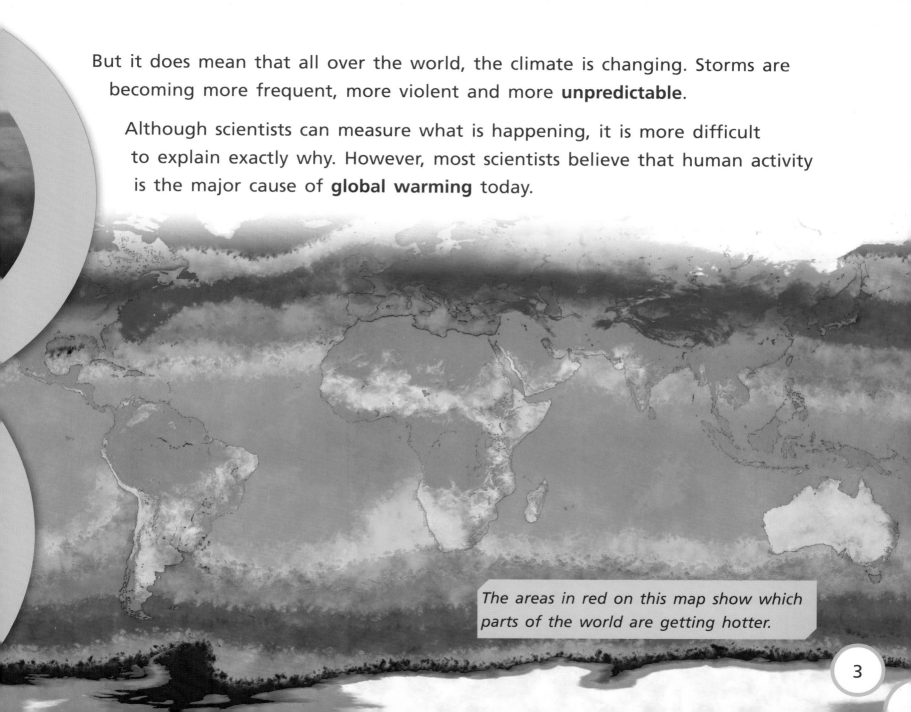

But it does mean that all over the world, the climate is changing. Storms are becoming more frequent, more violent and more **unpredictable**.

Although scientists can measure what is happening, it is more difficult to explain exactly why. However, most scientists believe that human activity is the major cause of **global warming** today.

The areas in red on this map show which parts of the world are getting hotter.

A **CHANGING** PLANET

Scientists know that the climate has changed a great deal on Earth over the 4.5 billion years it has existed. The changes happened very slowly, over millions of years. Today, big changes are happening so quickly, they are taking place within people's lifetimes. However, scientists need to look at what happened in the past to help understand clues about what might happen in the future.

The Earth is made up of different layers. Its crust is less than 100 kilometres thick. This crust floats on a molten centre.

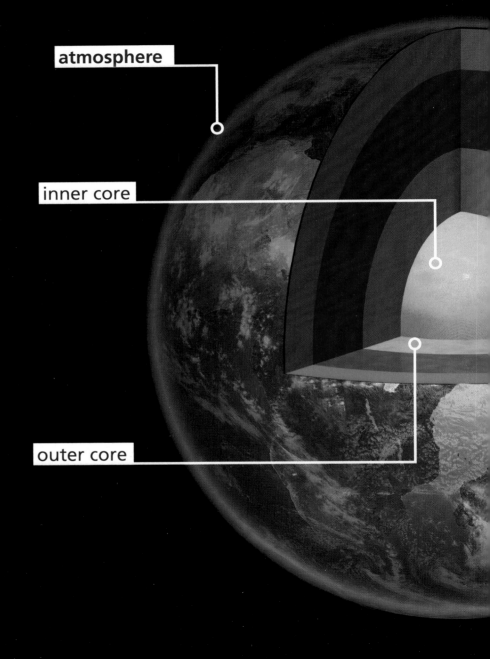

atmosphere

inner core

outer core

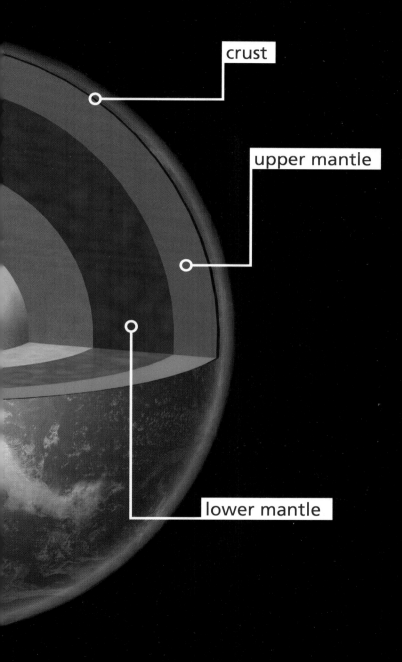

crust

upper mantle

lower mantle

A dynamic planet

The Earth is a very dynamic planet.
The forces of nature cause constant change to
the landscape and climate. The Earth is not solid
all the way through. The outer layer is the crust,
which carries all the land and the oceans.
The Earth's crust floats on layers of red-hot, molten
rock. The core is molten metal. Over millions
and millions of years, the land and the oceans
have slowly moved their positions. As they moved,
the climate on Earth has changed, too.

Through studying patterns of climate change,
scientists know that the Earth has already changed
several times during the distant past. Planet Earth
has been everything from Snowball Earth -
a freezing-cold place covered with ice - to Desert
Earth, a hot, dry world. The land has also been
covered by jungle and surrounded by warm seas.

LOOKING AT THE PAST

Millions of years ago, long before humans lived on the Earth, the climate was warmer and drier than it is today. Humans could not have survived in that climate.

There was also much more **carbon dioxide** (CO_2) and methane [mee- th- ain] in the atmosphere. Scientists believe that there was over six times as much carbon dioxide in the air as there is today. Carbon dioxide and methane are greenhouse gases. They help to make the climate hotter and drier.

It would have been much harder to breathe, because there was much less oxygen. All animals need oxygen to live and so it is perhaps not surprising that many animals died out.

At this time, all the **continents** were stuck together in one super-continent called Pangea (Pan-jee-ah).

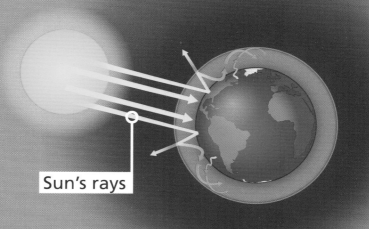

Sun's rays

WHAT IS A **GREENHOUSE GAS?**

A greenhouse gas allows the Sun's rays to pass through to the Earth, but does not allow the heat to escape. It is rather like sitting in a greenhouse in the full sun.

If there was less greenhouse gas in the atmosphere, the Earth would be much cooler.

DESERT EARTH

The world which the dinosaurs roamed 200 million years ago probably looked like this.

The Earth's crust has always moved. It is still moving. Slowly, very slowly, over millions and millions of years, the huge super-continent of Pangea began to break up.

The world was extremely hot and dry, with lots of deserts, as most land areas were far from the sea. The first dinosaurs roamed the Earth. This period of time is called the Triassic period and lasted about 40 million years.

The red arrows show the movement of the plates. This is how Pangea began to break up.

HOW DO **SCIENTISTS** KNOW ABOUT THE EARTH BEFORE **HUMANS EXISTED?**

Scientists know where and when the climate on Earth has been hot and dry because they have studied ancient rocks. The way that some rocks are formed shows that they were created in desert places. Similar rocks have been found in different parts of the world, helping scientists to understand how the continents broke away from each other. The rocks prove Pangea existed and broke apart.

A **JUNGLE-COVERED** WORLD

Over 180 million years ago, as Pangea broke up, the ocean filled the gaps between the continents. This meant the climate became wetter.

Warm, shallow seas surrounded the new continents. The conditions were perfect for all kinds of plants. Huge jungles grew. This was called the Jurassic Period. At this time, dinosaurs lived all over the world. Warm, wet jungles provided a perfect habitat for them. The Earth was much warmer than today.

Over the next 100 million years, dinosaurs were the most successful species on the warm planet. Then, about 70 million years ago, scientists think that meteors struck the Earth, creating a huge layer of dust in the atmosphere. This cut out the sun's rays and is believed to have killed the dinosaurs. The Earth became much colder. The effects of the meteor strike are believed to have been what killed the dinosaurs.

This is how scientists think the Earth may have looked during the Jurassic Period.

SNOWBALL EARTH

The climate on Earth is very sensitive. Over millions and millions of years, it can change in many ways and for many reasons. Scientists think that in the past, the Earth also became very cold. This is called an Ice Age.

As the plates on the Earth's crust move apart, the continents become separated by cool sea and the land temperatures begin to fall.
As it gets colder, the sea at the North and South Poles freezes into ice sheets. These spread across the land. An Ice Age begins. The plates move again and the climate gets warmer. The ice sheets melt and the Ice Age ends. Although it gets warmer, it is never hot enough for the ice to melt at the poles.

This process of warming up then cooling down has happened several times over millions of years, and each time it changes the climate.

North Pole

South Pole

The Ice Age meant animals had to adapt to the cold climate or die.

Scientists call these periods 'interglacials', or 'between ice ages'. The Earth is between ice ages at the moment and has been for about 11,000 years. The Earth's climate is not extremely cold, but it isn't very hot, either. This climate suits humans well.

Winners and Losers

In the past, when the Earth became very hot, lots of animals became extinct. They couldn't **adapt** to survive in the climate they found themselves in. When it became cold, some animals grew thick fur, and some grew an extra layer of fat to survive. Animals that couldn't adapt in this way became extinct. Humans discovered ways to live in the cooler climate and they were able to live all over the planet.

TODAY'S **WARMING WORLD**

In modern times, scientists think that the climate is changing in a different way. It is changing faster than ever before. Change is happening within one lifetime, not over millions of years. As the ice sheets and glaciers melt, the world is getting warmer and warmer and scientists can measure these changes.

How does melting ice make the Earth warmer?

There are fewer ice sheets and glaciers because they are melting. This means that less sunlight is reflected back into space. Sunlight warms the rocks where once there was ice and this makes even more ice melt.

As the ice melts, dead animals and plants which had been trapped in it thaw out and rot. When things rot, they create methane and carbon dioxide, powerful greenhouse gases. This has an effect, too.

As the Arctic gets warmer, the icy ground begins to melt. This is a rotting mammoth from the last Ice Age. It is in Siberia, Russia.

RISING SEA LEVELS

Ice at the North and South Poles is melting faster than ever before. The melted ice is flooding into the oceans, making sea levels rise all around the world.

Over the past 100 years, the average sea level has risen by 18 centimetres. Some scientists think that sea levels could rise by 1.5 metres or more by the year 2100.

In areas away from the coast, rises in sea levels might not be so serious, but for people who live in low-lying areas or on islands, the result could be disastrous. Many big cities are close to the sea. In the future, many places like New York, London, Amsterdam, Mumbai and Guangzhou could become flooded.

London could be flooded if sea levels continue to rise. This illustration shows what it might look like.

As the Earth gets warmer, storms will get stronger and more destructive.

WHAT HAPPENS AS THE **WORLD** GETS **WARMER**?

As the Earth warms, weather patterns are changing. Some places are getting hotter and drier. New deserts are forming. Some places are getting stormier and wetter. There are more floods. A few places are even getting cooler.

How will the climate change?

Many hot places will become cooler and many cold places may get warmer. This happens because the water in the seas and oceans is changing temperature and affecting the temperature on the land.

The direction of the wind is also changing because of the changes in temperature. The winds carry water across the land in clouds. This becomes rain. Winds are not reaching the same places at the same times of the year. Farmers will be affected by changes in the ways that the wind travels around the world.

Big storms, called typhoons or hurricanes, develop over the sea. As the sea gets warmer, storms become much bigger and stronger.

HAVE **HUMANS** CAUSED **GLOBAL WARMING**?

Weather and climate systems are very complex and sensitive. This means the slightest change to the planet, or the way humans live, can have a huge effect on the climate.

Over the past 30 years, scientists have proved that human activity is a major cause of global warming and climate change. But it is not only the fault of humans. Scientists do not yet fully understand all the causes.

How does the burning of trees increase global warming?
Fires produce carbon dioxide. There are also fewer trees to cool the planet.

How does burning fossil fuels increase global warming?
Fossil fuels, like coal, gas and oil, produce carbon dioxide (CO_2) when burnt. This then acts as a powerful greenhouse gas.

How do animals increase global warming?
When grass-fed animals digest their food, they produce methane. A single cow can emit enough methane in a day to run a laptop.

How does water vapour increase global warming?
As water warms, it becomes a gas. This gas rises up in the atmosphere and traps the heat, as greenhouse gases do.

Vapour becomes cloud.

Cloud traps heat.

Trapped heat continues to warm the Earth.

Water vapour rises.

WHAT DO **PEOPLE** SAY ABOUT **GLOBAL WARMING**?

Not everyone agrees about what is happening to the climate. What are the arguments? How do scientists respond to these arguments?

The world has had many periods of warming and cooling in its history. This has happened entirely naturally.

Scientists say: the difference between what is happening now and what happened in the past, is that it is happening much, much faster. We have proof that burning fossil fuels causes greenhouse gases. Greenhouse gases make the Earth warmer. We know that global warming began soon after people began to burn lots of fossil fuels.

Does it matter if the world gets hotter? The world has been hotter before and it is still here.

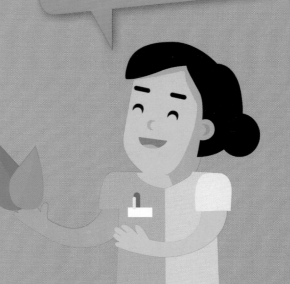

Scientists say: but how long can humans wait for it to cool down? It took millions of years in the past. When the world got hotter, lots of animals died out as they couldn't adapt. We need to adapt today.

HOW CAN WE MAKE ELECTRICITY IN **THE FUTURE**?

Electricity is used for everything: lighting, heating, industry, transport, communications. People will still need electricity in the near future. In the past, electricity was made by burning fossil fuels, such as gas and coal. This produces huge amounts of greenhouse gases. How can the way electricity is made be changed?

Renewable energy

In the last few years, scientists have discovered that electricity can be made in ways that don't produce many greenhouse gases and don't waste natural **resources**. This 'renewable energy' is made by using resources which are unlikely to run out in the near future; heat from inside the sun, power from waves, tides, or wind, or heat from the Earth.

CREATING **RENEWABLE ENERGY**

Renewable energy is made by taking energy from a natural source and storing it as electricity. At the moment, renewable energy is very expensive to make. Scientists need to do a lot more research to make it work efficiently.

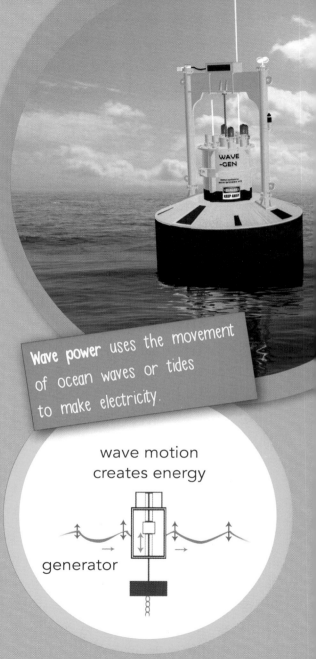

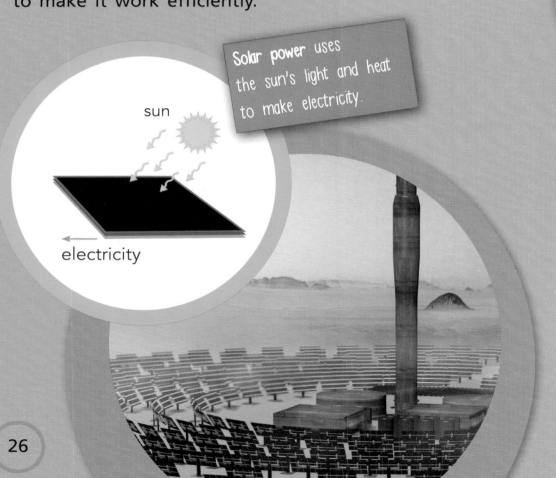

Solar power uses the sun's light and heat to make electricity.

sun

electricity

Wave power uses the movement of ocean waves or tides to make electricity.

wave motion creates energy

generator

WAVE -GEN

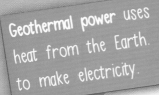

Geothermal power uses heat from the Earth to make electricity.

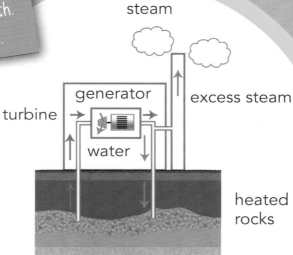

steam

generator

excess steam

turbine

water

heated rocks

rocks holding hot water or steam

NUCLEAR ENERGY

Nuclear energy produces a lot of power, but some scientists do not think that it can be used safely yet. More research is needed. Nuclear energy also produces a lot of dangerous **waste**.

Hydro-electric power uses the energy made by water running downhill to turn turbines.

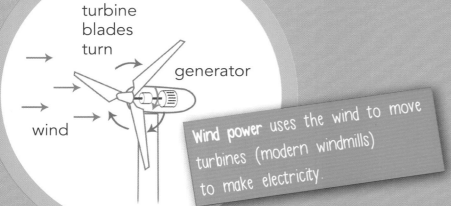

turbine blades turn

generator

wind

Wind power uses the wind to move turbines (modern windmills) to make electricity.

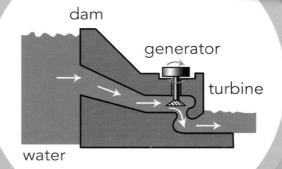

dam

generator

turbine

water

NEW WAYS OF **LIVING**

People need to design new and more efficient ways of making homes, growing food and travelling.

Cities need to be planned to cope with rising sea levels, and transport will have to become non-polluting, or 'clean', instead of relying on fossil fuels like oil, petrol or diesel.

People might find new ways to live, like building cities on the water.

In the future, this may be how people grow vegetables.

As the population increases, and land becomes scarce due to flooding and **drought**, farms will need to use less space to grow food. Resources will have to be managed much better. Perhaps scientists will learn how to grow food in the sea.

Even more efficient ways to make energy need to be found. But these changes can't be made overnight.

It is very difficult for people to change the way they live. They may not be able to eat, work and live in the same way as they are used to. Some creatures will become extinct, as the dinosaurs did many millions of years ago. People need to plan and adapt if they are to survive in a changing climate.

GLOSSARY

adapt   change to suit the environment

atmosphere   layers of gases that surround the Earth

continents   large areas of land, such as Africa or Asia

carbon dioxide   colourless gas in the atmosphere

drought   when little rain falls

global warming   process by which the Earth is getting warmer

resources   things that can be used. Renewable
   resources can be used over and over again, like
   wind and water and heat from the sun

unpredictable   unable to know what will happen

waste   rubbish

INDEX

The Changing Climate ⬤ Jon Hughes

Teaching notes written by Glen Franklin and Sue Bodman

Using this book

Content/theme/subject

This book explores the facts and opinions surrounding climate change: an important topic around the world. Going back to pre-historic times, the book tracks the changing climates the world has experienced, and discusses the potential impacts of global warming on the world today.

Language structure

- Sentences are of greater complexity, and include multiple clauses: *'scientists need to look at what happened in the past to help understand clues about what might happen in the future'* (p.4).

- Appropriate technical vocabulary and language structure is used for the message being given and received, such as in the question and answer dialogue between members of the public and the scientists on pp.22 and 23.

Book structure/visual features

- A range of appropriate non-fiction features are employed, including diagrams to explain more complex scientific concepts.

- A mix of chronological and non-chronological reporting is used to explain the historical perspective and the current position of climate change.

Vocabulary and comprehension

- The language of causality (*'This happens because the water in the seas and oceans is changing temperature and affecting the temperature on the land.' p.26*) and of persuasion (*'people need to plan and adapt if they are to survive in a changing climate'*, p.29) is used to position the reader and convey the author's message.

- Diagrams, captions and labels support the main text, adding further information to support the reader's comprehension.

Curriculum links

Science – There are many different science investigations related to global warming. For example, children could collect data to chart the temperature of different countries across a period of time, using information from the internet to compare with the average temperature for the time of year.

Humanities – Children could investigate places around the world which are affected by the impact of climate change, such as flooding in Bangladesh or drought in parts of the Africa. Look at how people in these lands are finding ways to adapt to the changing conditions.

Learning outcomes

Children can:

- locate relevant information in the text and present this is an appropriate form for a given audience

- express personal responses to text, such as considering the usefulness and clarity of certain features

- consider whether statements are fact or opinion, and identify evidence in the text which supports their decision.

Planning for guided reading

Lesson One: *Effectiveness of non-fiction features*

Give a copy of the book to each child, and ask them to read the title, blurb and pp.2-3 quietly to themselves. Discuss what the book is about. Consider the impact of the powerful opening sentence on p.2: (*'2016 was the hottest year ever recorded'*), noting the immediacy and engagement with the reader from the outset. Explore this two-page spread, looking at the various non-fiction text features employed. For example, there are two glossary words on p.3. Go to the glossary and read the definitions provided there. Discuss with the children how effective these are in helping ascertain the meaning of the text on p.3. Look at the map, also on p.3. Explore the caption. Discuss how the map helps the reader understand the point being made.

Turn to pp.4-5. Consider how this diagram is different. Ask: *Why do you think the author decided to use a diagram here?* Draw out from the children how diagrams can help the reader understand complex ideas and theories. Consider the meaning of the heading on p.5: *'A dynamic planet'*. In pairs, ask the children to read the text on pp.4-5, and then discuss how helpful they found the diagram in supporting their reading of this page, and their understanding of the concept of the planet being dynamic.